LIGHTNING BOLT BOOKS™

Meet a Baby Chimpanzee

Mari Schuh

Lerner Publications
Minneapolis

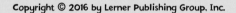

Content Consultant: Dr. Mark C. Andersen, Department of Fish Wildlife and Conservation Ecology, New Mexico State University

Lerner Publications Company
A division of Lerner Publishing Group, Inc.
241 First Avenue North
Minneapolis, MN 55401 USA

For reading levels and more information, look up this title at www.lernerbooks.com.

Library of Congress Cataloging-in-Publication Data

Schuh, Mari C., 1975–.
    Meet a baby chimpanzee / Mari Schuh.
    pages cm. — (Lightning bolt books. Baby African animals)
    Includes index.
    Audience: Ages 5–8.
    Audience: Grades K to 3.
    ISBN 978-1-4677-7973-9 7(lb : alk. paper) — ISBN 978-1-4677-8357-6 (pb : alk. paper) — ISBN 978-1-4677-8358-3 (eb pdf)
    1. Chimpanzees—Infancy—Juvenile literature. I. Title.
QL737.P94S38 2015
599.8851′39—dc23   2015005817

Manufactured in the United States of America
1 – BP – 7/15/15

Table of Contents

Life as a Baby Chimpanzee

A mother chimpanzee is about to give birth. Her baby grew inside her for around eight months. Now the baby is ready to be born. The mother gives birth alone.

Sometimes mother chimpanzees give birth to twins.

Newborn chimpanzees are smaller than most newborn human babies.

Baby chimpanzees are small. They weigh about 4 pounds (2 kilograms). Mother chimpanzees weigh 70 to 100 pounds (32 to 45 kg). That is almost as much as a human teenager might weigh.

Baby chimpanzees do not look exactly like their parents. They do not have as much hair. Baby chimpanzees are born with pink faces.

Baby chimps have white tufts of hair on their bottoms.

As the babies get bigger, they grow long, dark hair.

As chimpanzees grow, they will look more like their parents. The chimpanzees' faces get darker.

Chimpanzees are social animals. They live in communities with fifteen or more chimpanzees. They form smaller groups within these communities.

The chimpanzees in a community break off into smaller social groups.

Female chimpanzees move from community to community. They do not stay with one group for long.

Female chimpanzees often move from place to place.

Learning and Changing

A baby chimpanzee stays with its mother for many years. It drinks her milk and sleeps with her.

At five months old, the baby chimp is strong enough to ride on its mother's back.

After turning two years old, baby chimps begin climbing around. But they do not go far.

Baby chimps get bigger each year.

By three years old, baby chimps weigh around 18 pounds (8 kg). They are about the size of a small dog.

Chimps learn to walk at about age four. They walk on their knuckles for support. Their arms are longer than their legs.

Chimpanzees sometimes walk on all four limbs.

Baby chimpanzees have a long childhood. They need many years to learn how to be independent.

Chimpanzees learn lots of things from their mothers.

14

Chimpanzees pick dirt and bugs out of one another's hair.

Baby chimps copy their mothers. They learn how to groom other chimps. This helps chimpanzees make friends.

Gathering Food

A baby chimp learns about food from its mother. Finding and eating food takes a long time. They search together for hours.

A mother and her baby search the trees for food.

A mother chimp eats fruit, leaves, bugs, stems, and bark. The baby chimp watches its mother closely.

Baby chimps sniff their mothers' food.

Chimps need their mothers' milk for many years.

Baby chimps drink only their mothers' milk at first. But around five months old, a baby chimp tries small bites of its mother's food.

After age two, a baby chimp starts eating more solid food. It nibbles on fruits and plants.

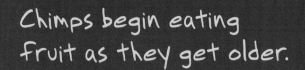

Chimps begin eating fruit as they get older.

A baby chimp no longer needs its mother's milk at five years old. It has learned where to find ripe fruit.

This chimp has learned which foods are safe to eat.

Chimpanzees use leaves as sponges.

Mother chimps also teach their babies how to get water. They use leaves to soak up water from holes in trees.

Growing Up

A young chimp explores the treetops.

As a chimpanzee grows, it spends less time with its mother. It explores the rain forests and woodlands.

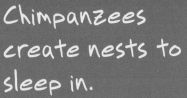
Chimpanzees create nests to sleep in.

By age five, a young chimp is ready to sleep alone. It finds branches and leaves in the forest. It bends the branches to make a nest at night.

Chimps get stronger as they grow. They move quickly through the forest. Around age seven, chimps are independent. They can take care of themselves.

Chimps swing from the trees with their strong arms.

Rocks help chimpanzees crack open nuts.

Chimpanzees learn how to use tools. They use sticks to get bugs out of nests.

They use leaves to clean their bodies.

Mothers teach their babies how to live in the rain forest.

Many female chimpanzees become mothers around age thirteen. They have one baby every four or five years.

Male chimpanzees are adults around age sixteen. Chimpanzees can live for forty to fifty years in the wild.

Chimpanzee Life Cycle

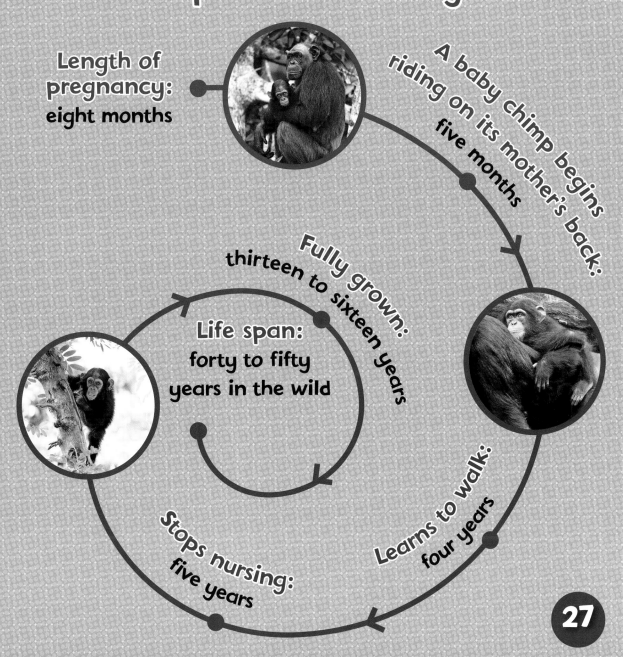

Length of pregnancy: eight months

A baby chimp begins riding on its mother's back: five months

Fully grown: thirteen to sixteen years

Life span: forty to fifty years in the wild

Learns to walk: four years

Stops nursing: five years

Habitat in Focus

- Chimpanzees eat lots of fruit as they travel through their forest habitats. The fruits' seeds pass through the chimpanzees and into the soil. Then new plants grow in different places.

- People cut down trees in chimpanzee habitats. Smaller rain forests mean chimps have fewer places to live.

- Chimpanzees are endangered. They are in danger of dying out. But some people are working to save them and their forest homes.

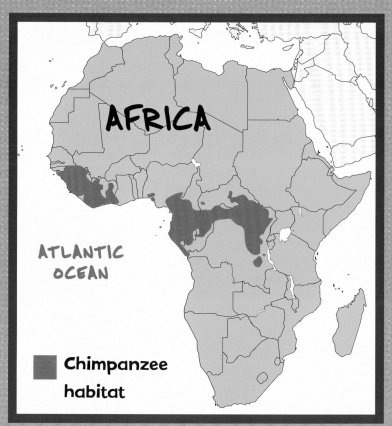

AFRICA

ATLANTIC OCEAN

■ Chimpanzee habitat

Fun Facts

- Chimpanzees take care of themselves when they are sick or hurt. They know which plants to use as medicine to get better.

- People can teach chimpanzees to use sign language.

- Chimpanzees are not monkeys. They are apes. Monkeys have tails, but apes do not.

- Chimpanzees kiss, tickle, and hug one another.

Glossary

community: a large group of chimpanzees

groom: to clean and take care of

independent: able to take care of yourself

rain forest: a thick area of trees where a lot of rain falls

ripe: fully grown and ready to be eaten

woodland: land covered with trees and bushes

Further Reading

Albee, Sarah. *Chimpanzees.* Pleasantville, NY: Gareth Stevens, 2010.

Carr, Aaron. *I Am a Chimpanzee.* New York: Av2 by Weigl, 2013.

Enchanted Learning: All about Chimpanzees http://www.enchantedlearning.com/subjects/apes/chimp

Greenberg, Daniel A., and Christina Wilsdon. *Chimpanzees.* New York: Marshall Cavendish Benchmark, 2010.

National Geographic Kids: Chimpanzee http://kids.nationalgeographic.com/content/kids/en_US/animals/chimpanzee

Owen, Ruth. *Chimpanzees.* New York: Windmill Books, 2012.

Spilsbury, Richard, and Louise Spilsbury. *Chimpanzee Troops.* New York: PowerKids, 2013.

Index

Photo Acknowledgments

The images in this book are used with the permission of: © Abeselom Zerit/ Shutterstock Images, pp. 2, 24; © Danita Delimont/Alamy, p. 4; © Sergey Uryadnikov/ Shutterstock Images, pp. 5, 27 (top); © SuperStock/Glow Images, p. 6; © ImpalaStock/ iStock/Thinkstock, p. 7; © Stephen Meese/Shutterstock Images, p. 8; © Foto Mous/ Shutterstock Images, p. 9; © Kitch Bain/Shutterstock Images, pp. 10, 27 (bottom right); © Kristof Degreef/Shutterstock Images, p. 11; © Leon P./Shutterstock Images, p. 12; © Nick Biemans/Shutterstock Images, pp. 13, 14, 31; © Tom Brakefield/Stockbyte/ Thinkstock, p. 15; © Ryan M. Bolton/Shutterstock Images, p. 16; © grass-lifeisgood/ Shutterstock Images, p. 17; © Holger Ehlers Naturephoto/Alamy, p. 18; © Sam D'Cruz/ Shutterstock Images, p. 19; © Anup Shah/Digital Vision/Thinkstock, p. 20; © TanzanianImages/iStock/Thinkstock, p. 21; © Worakit Sirijinda/Shutterstock Images, pp. 22, 27 (bottom left); © Kristin Mosher/Danita Delimont Photography/Newscom, p. 23; © zahorec/Shutterstock Images, p. 25; © Cuson/Shutterstock Images, p. 26; Red Line Editorial, p. 28; © Eric Isselee/iStock/Thinkstock, p. 30.

Front cover: Suzi Eszterhas/Minden Pictures/Newscom.

Main body text set in Johann Light 30/36.